SYMBOLS OF AMERICA

THE LIBERTY BELL

BY MARIA NELSON

Gareth Stevens
PUBLISHING

Please visit our website, www.garethstevens.com. For a free color catalog of all our high-quality books, call toll free 1-800-542-2595 or fax 1-877-542-2596.

Library of Congress Cataloging-in-Publication Data

Nelson, Maria.
The Liberty Bell / by Maria Nelson.
p. cm. — (Symbols of America)
Includes index.
ISBN 978-1-4824-1871-2 (pbk.)
ISBN 978-1-4824-1869-9 (6-pack)
ISBN 978-1-4824-1870-5 (library binding)
1. Liberty Bell — Juvenile literature. I. Nelson, Maria. II. Title.
F158.8.I3 N45 2015
974.8—d23

Published in 2015 by
Gareth Stevens Publishing
111 East 14th Street, Suite 349
New York, NY 10003

Designer: Sarah Liddell
Editor: Kristen Rajczak

Photo credits: Cover, pp. 1, 5 f11photo/Shutterstock.com; p. 7 Reverend Samuel Manning/The Bridgeman Art Library/Getty Images; p. 9 Rebekah McBride/Shutterstock.com; p. 11 UniversalImagesGroup/Contributor/Universal Images Group/Getty Images; p. 13 SuperStock/SuperStock/Getty Images; p. 15 Arthur Wong/Shutterstock.com; p. 17 YANGCHAO/Shutterstock.com; p. 19 Popperfoto/Contributor/Popperfoto/Getty Images; p. 21 Edwin Verin/Shutterstock.com.

Printed in the United States of America

CPSIA compliance information: Batch #CW15GS: For further information contact Gareth Stevens, New York, New York at 1-800-542-2595.

CONTENTS

Boldface words appear in the glossary.

Creating Symbols

Throughout the history of the United States, **liberty** has been very important. But since liberty can't be seen, people have come to know certain objects or places as **symbols** of it. The Liberty Bell is one such symbol.

The First Bell

In 1751, a bell was ordered for the State House in Philadelphia, Pennsylvania. The bell was **cast** in London, England. It weighed more than 2,000 pounds (908 kg)! After arriving in Pennsylvania in 1753, the bell was rung, and it cracked!

The Second and Third Bells

Philadelphia craftsmen John Pass and John Stow used the metal from this bell to make a new one. The sound of the second bell was poor, so the bell was cast again. It was then hung in the Pennsylvania State House.

9

The Revolution

The bell was rung to bring people together for announcements and events. It was rung at the start of the **American Revolution** in 1775. Then, the bell was rung before the first public reading of the Declaration of Independence on July 8, 1776.

The bell was taken from Philadelphia to Allentown, Pennsylvania, when British soldiers were marching on the city in 1777. When the war was over, the bell was returned. It was then rung on July 4 and other important days.

Cracked Again!

The bell started to crack when it was rung in 1835. When it rung for George Washington's birthday in 1846, the crack grew. The bell could no longer ring properly. Since then, it's only been tapped on special occasions.

15

The Liberty Bell

A line about liberty is written on the bell. Knowing this, those against slavery began to call it the Liberty Bell around 1839. It became a symbol of freedom for the first time.

LET FREEDOM RING 17

The Liberty Bell traveled around the United States after the **Civil War**. It was meant to bring the country together. Later, other groups looking for more freedoms would use the bell as a symbol.

See the Bell

The Liberty Bell no longer hangs in the State House, now known as Independence Hall. It has its own building that you can visit! The millions of people who visit it every year are reminded of the importance of our freedom.

LIBERTY BELL TIMELINE

1751
A bell is ordered for the Pennsylvania State House.

1835
The bell starts to crack.

1775
The bell is rung at the start of the American Revolution.

1846
The bell cracks beyond repair. It's rung for the last time.

1776
The bell is rung at the first public reading of the Declaration of Independence.

1753
The bell cracks. It's made into a new bell.

1839
The name "Liberty Bell" is first used.

GLOSSARY

American Revolution: the war in which the colonies won their freedom from England

cast: to make an object by pouring melted matter into a mold and letting it harden

Civil War: a war fought from 1861 to 1865 in the United States between the Union (the Northern states) and the Confederacy (the Southern states)

liberty: freedom

symbol: a picture, object, or shape that stands for something else

FOR MORE INFORMATION

BOOKS

Eldridge, Alison, and Stephen Eldridge. *The Liberty Bell: An American Symbol.* Berkeley Heights, NJ: Enslow Elementary, 2012.

Rustad, Martha E. H. *Can We Ring the Liberty Bell?* Minneapolis, MN: Millbrook Press, 2014.

WEBSITES

Liberty Bell Center
www.nps.gov/inde/liberty-bell-center.htm
Plan a visit to the Liberty Bell using this website.

Symbols of US Government: The Liberty Bell
bensguide.gpo.gov/3-5/symbols/libertybell.html
Read more about the history of the Liberty Bell.

INDEX